Battling the Beast:
Growing in Faith through Cancer

by Katy Huth Jones

All rights reserved. No part of this publication may be reproduced or transmitted in any form or by any means, electronic or mechanical, including photocopy, recording, or any information and retrieval system, without the prior written permission of the publisher, except the case of brief quotations for reviews. No part of this book may be scanned, uploaded, or distributed via the Internet without the publisher's permission, and is a violation of International copyright law and subjects the violator to severe fines and/or imprisonment.

Battling the Beast: Growing in Faith through Cancer

Copyright © 2018 by Katy Huth Jones

ISBN 13: 978-1-7310-1337-8

Published in the United States of America

First print edition: November 2018 by Quinlan Creek Press

Cover image: canva.com

Sword image: pixabay.com

Scripture quotations from The Authorized (King James) Version. Rights in the Authorized Version in the United Kingdom are vested in the Crown. Reproduced by permission of the Crown's patentee, Cambridge University Press.

Unless otherwise indicated, all Scripture quotations are from The ESV® Bible (The Holy Bible, English Standard Version®), copyright © 2001 by Crossway, a publishing ministry of Good News Publishers. Used by permission. All rights reserved.

The hymn, "Thou Thinkest, Lord, of Me," by Edmund Simon Lorenz (1885) is in the Public Domain.

The hymn, "In Heavenly Love Abiding," by Anna Letitia Waring (1850) is in the Public Domain.

Dedication

This book is dedicated to Keith,
my best friend and husband for forty years.
His unswerving love and support during this
cancer journey has been a huge encouragement
and source of strength,
second only to God, our Rock.

Table of Contents

Chapter		Page
1	Getting Another Opinion	1
2	Care and Comfort of the Saints	4
3	Three Little Words	6
4	The Need for Comfort	8
5	The Important Things of Life	10
6	A Council of War	13
7	The Power of the Mind	16
8	Control is an Illusion	19
9	The Power of Prayer	21
10	Thankful for Every Small Victory	23
11	Who Stole My Brain?	26
12	God's Hand through the Fire	29
13	Love in Action	32
14	When Marriage Vows Become Real	35
15	Preparing for Battle	37
16	Losing My Glory	39
17	The Hour of Dread	42
18	Producing Steadfastness	44
19	Practicing Good Medicine	47
20	Strange Weapons	49
21	Renewing Determination	52
22	Sentenced to Jail	54
23	What Love Looks Like	57
24	Getting Restless	59
25	Encouragement	62
26	Plans	65

27	Death and Life	68
28	Into the Darkness	71
29	Waiting is SO Hard!	73
30	Understanding = Compassion	75
31	About Chemotherapy	78
32	Anticipation and Anxiety	81
33	How Do You Spell Relief?	83
	Afterwards	85

Introduction

This is the book I wish I could have found when I first faced non-Hodgkin's lymphoma at age 46 and was desperately looking for someone who was still alive more than five years later.

What I did find in my cancer journey was even more important:

- A deeper trust and faith in God my Father.

- The ability to savor each moment of life rather than rush through each day unmindful of His blessings.

- To rest my hope in my Lord Jesus Christ and be able to honestly say I look forward to going home someday.

The dated entries are a series of emails I sent to a group of homeschooling Christian moms I'd been a part of since 1995. After each email is additional information, followed by a Scripture and a reflection upon what I was learning in a painful, indelible way during the months of January, February, March, and April, 2005.

A special thanks goes to my husband Keith, who was my rock during all these scary procedures and side effects. Our older son David was in college in Florida that semester and managed to graduate in May while supporting me long distance. Our younger son Robert, only fourteen when our lives were rocked by a cancer diagnosis, was the best possible helper while keeping up with his schoolwork, trumpet practice, and art, winning a "People's Choice Award" for one of his paintings at a local art gallery.

My hope as you read this is that you will come to lean upon God through this journey you did not choose to make. May your faith enable you to encourage others who have joined this unexpected "club" of survivors.

"Blessed be the God and Father of our Lord Jesus Christ, the Father of mercies and God of all comfort, who comforts us in all our affliction, so that we may be able to comfort those who are in any affliction, with the comfort with which we ourselves are comforted by God."

II Corinthians 1:3-4

Reflection: Our suffering teaches us to understand how others feel when they suffer, and also shows us how to comfort them.

Chapter 1
Getting Another Opinion

January 6: Dear sisters, I went to a new doctor this afternoon and I am having surgery Monday morning to remove this lymph node that keeps growing, so much so that it's putting pressure on my esophagus and carotid artery. I will just be glad to know something definite. The doctor said he should have results next Thursday—he's concerned it may be Hodgkin's. I also sliced my hand yesterday evening while opening a pop-top can of soup, but by the time the ER doctor got to me (busy evening) I managed to get the bleeding stopped so he didn't suture it. Now I wish he had. I had to tape my thumb before I went to bed because every time I move it the wound starts to split at the edges. It's not big, just deep and barely above the webbing between my thumb and first finger, so now it's hard not to move it!

On a funnier note, I misplaced my glasses at noon looking for a bowl to put our new hermit crab in, so I had to go to homeschool bowling and the doctor with NO glasses! Just a little while ago, I found my glasses—on the shelf INSIDE the cabinet where I keep my plastic bowls! "Of all the things I've lost, I miss my mind the most…"

* * *

I'd known something was wrong for nine months. After a bad sinus infection in March 2004, the enlarged lymph nodes in my neck did not reduce. Soon I began having off-and-on low grade fevers and chills, night sweats, and feeling more exhausted than I'd ever felt before (malaise). I looked it up on the internet and realized I had every symptom of lymphoma except the one I wouldn't mind having, weight loss.

I went to three different doctors over the next few months and had many tests and a needle biopsy of the largest lymph node, which came back inconclusive. The doctors said I had an infection or menopausal symptoms. Not until my sister was diagnosed with non-Hodgkin's lymphoma that December, did I realize I needed to find a fourth doctor and find out once and for all what was going on.

"The simple believes everything, but the prudent gives thought to his steps."

Proverbs 14:15

Reflection: Don't ignore potential bad news, hoping it will go away. Even if a doctor tells you there's nothing wrong, you know your body better than he or she does, and should get another opinion if something feels wrong inside.

Chapter 2

Care and Comfort for the Saints

January 10: Surgery update: I had an Easter egg! Thought that would get your attention! That's what the doctor told my husband—that my lymph node was like a huge Easter egg as long as his thumb! I knew I couldn't be imagining it in there. Anyway, I'm wearing this stylish "wimple" to support my neck, and it's pretty sore, but I'm finally getting undrowsy. I'll find out the results of the path report on Thursday. I haven't seen the incision yet so hopefully it's not too yucky!

Thank you SO much for all the prayers! Just knowing so many were praying helped me stay totally calm! And two of my dear sisters in Christ brought food for us today, one for lunch and the other for supper, and they both brought chicken & dumplings. Yummy, though I can't chew very well right now.

* * *

This surgery was supposed to be under local anesthesia, since lymph nodes are normally the size of a pea. But when I woke up after general anesthesia, the doctor explained that because the lymph node was pressing on my carotid artery, he had to "knock me out" so he wouldn't risk nicking it. He also said the lymph node was hard and broke in half. At that moment, I knew it wouldn't be good news.

"Bear one another's burdens, and so fulfill the law of Christ."

Galatians 6:2

Reflection: In addition to praying for the sick and suffering, the practical help of providing food for the patient and family seems a small thing but is a great comfort. I'd done so for others in the past, but never realized what a blessing it was until I was the recipient. As one of my friends put it, "You have blessed us, now let us have the privilege of blessing you."

Chapter 3
Three Little Words

January 13: Bad news ☹ I just got back from the doctor's office. I'm not surprised, really, but I was sure hoping it would turn out benign. I do have lymphoma but I'll have to have a CT scan to know for sure how bad. If it's spread I'll have to have chemo; if it hasn't I may just have radiation. Please keep me in your prayers, dear sisters! Right now I'm kind of stunned. I still haven't told my parents or my in-laws. I've got to figure out how to do that without getting them too upset. My younger sister started radiation yesterday for her lymphoma. How weird is that? The doctor did say it tended to run in families….

The Lord has seen me through many things, and I know He will hold me through this, too. Thank you, ladies, for being there.

* * *

It's the ultimate of pivotal moments when you hear three little words that forever change your life: "You have cancer." One moment you are the person you've always been, and the next, you're a cancer patient. The doctor was amazed that I didn't cry, that I stayed calm when he gave me the diagnosis. For me, it was more relief than surprise. I explained to him I'd suspected it for some time. Now that the Beast had a name, a plan of attack could be made.

"For the righteous will never be moved; he will be remembered forever. He is not afraid of bad news; his heart is firm, trusting in the LORD."

Psalm 112:6-7

Reflection: A spectrum of emotion passes through you like a lightning bolt: shock, disbelief, horror, despair, anger. Cancer is what happens to *other* people! You cry, you scream, you ask God, "Why me?" But eventually, you have to come to a place of acceptance. There is no understanding. There is no why. There is only humble resignation.

And then follows a strong desire to live and NOT die.

Chapter 4
The Need for Comfort

January 16: You ladies are the best! Just knowing you are praying is helping me stay calm SO much! I feel like I'm having to reassure so many others right now, but I do feel very calm and totally reassured that the Lord is with me, no matter what happens. His grace really IS sufficient... (II Corinthians 12:9: "My grace is sufficient for thee, for My strength is made perfect in weakness...")

My mother usually controls her language around me, but when I told her she kinda "slipped", but I managed to get her calmed down. My mother-in-law also started crying, but seeing me calm helped her calm down, too.

The worst is not knowing what's going to happen next, how many "ouchies" I'm going to have to endure. But I'm gonna try to use this as an opportunity to grow in faith...and yes, slow down.

Please keep those prayers coming, and I'll let you know as soon as I know something more. I see the cancer doctor on the 28th after all the test results are in.

* * *

One of the most surprising things about having to tell people I had cancer was *their* reaction to the news. I thought I would be receiving comfort from others, but I found myself having to comfort *them*. The reactions ranged from shock to horror to disbelief. Some gave unwanted advice. Some told me horror stories about others they'd known who'd died from cancer. Others withdrew completely from me. Within a short time I realized most people have NO idea what to say to someone who has contracted this dreadful disease that everyone dreads. And, I regretfully realized, I had on occasion said the very same things.

"Even though I walk through the valley of the shadow of death, I will fear no evil, for you are with me; your rod and your staff, they comfort me."

Psalm 23:4

Reflection: Sometimes we can't find comfort where we think we will, but we can always find comfort in our Shepherd, our faithful heavenly Father.

Chapter 5

The Important Things of Life

January 24: I'm going TOMORROW! I was going to have to wait until Friday to see the cancer doctor, but they had a cancellation and so I'm going tomorrow morning! I'm really nervous now, even though I'm VERY glad I don't have to wait until Friday.

My life will never be the same again, but actually I think that will be a very good thing! There's nothing like staring early death in the face to help you see what life is truly about!

I have no doubt that God is with me, and that one of my greatest blessings is knowing you wonderful ladies!

* * *

My life was crazy before my diagnosis. I homeschooled my son as well as other students in co-op classes, directed a homeschool band, taught private flute at the local middle school and high school, taught Bible classes, was a Boy scout leader, and worked as a freelance writer for magazines. Every minute of every day was scheduled like a club sandwich. I got some weird kind of "high" being able to juggle so many things simultaneously without dropping any of them. All that came to a screeching halt. What a shock! The realization that life could go on without me, that I was not irreplaceable, was even more of a shock than hearing I had cancer.

"Come now, you who say, 'Today or tomorrow we will go into such and such a town and spend a year there and trade and make a profit'—yet you do not know what tomorrow will bring. What is your life? For you are a mist that appears for a little time and then vanishes."

James 4:13-14

Reflection: A cancer diagnosis showed me that I was running in circles on a hamster wheel. Even though everything I did was something profitable for someone, I was neglecting to focus my heart and my energy on spiritual things. I needed to learn that no matter what happens, life goes on, and God will take care of us.

Chapter 6
A Council of War

January 25: Good news/bad news: My head is spinning right now, and my hip is very sore from a bone marrow biopsy—it felt like the doctor stuck tweezers into my hip bone. The good news is that it is NOT the uncurable kind of lymphoma!

The bad news is that it is a large mass of intermediate to high grade (fast growing) non-Hodgkin's lymphoma but seems to be Stage 1, in my neck; the bone marrow biopsy is to make sure it isn't in the blood, which would make it Stage IV. Tomorrow (Wednesday) I will have a port catheter inserted in my chest and hooked up to the large vein because I begin chemotherapy next week. On Thursday I have some kind of heart scan to make sure there are no problems there before they actually start the chemo. On Tuesday I will have IV Rituxan, which is an immunotherapy drug that attaches to the cancer cells and "marks" them for destruction (sounds pretty cool to me!) On Thursday I will have the chemo "cocktail" with 3 different drugs. I will take Prednisone orally for five days (which helps the other stuff work its best). The next two weeks after that I will have blood tests to keep an eye on this process, and repeat the cycle at least 3 more times. I may or may not need radiation after that, or could get 2 more rounds of chemo, depending on what the CT scan shows.

The good news is that I WILL get to go to Florida on May 5th to see David get his BA (the doctor put that date in the chart and promised me I would be able to go, but I would be bald! I told her I will just have to wear a stylish hat!)

The other good news is that this type of lymphoma, while pretty scary, has the potential to be cured, so please keep those prayers coming! I am SO relieved to finally know exactly what is going on and to have a PLAN of action! (The cancer doctor was pretty aggravated with the ENT who didn't catch it last summer, but she says we still caught it in time. She's a good person to have on YOUR side! I really like her!)

Anyway, this will not be pleasant, but it's definitely doable. Thank you SO much for your concern and your prayers! You all are the best!

* * *

My oncologist, Dr. B, asked if I wanted a referral to M.D. Anderson for a second opinion. She exuded confidence in the treatment of lymphoma, and I told her I didn't feel the need for a second opinion. I was relieved to be able to do everything in our relatively small town without having to drive an hour to the nearest big city.

"Plans are established by counsel; by wise guidance wage war."

Proverbs 20:18

Reflection: Fighting cancer IS a battle: physical, mental, emotional, and spiritual. It's important to have a "general" you are confident can help you defeat the Beast, while also remembering God is the Supreme Commander in this war.

Chapter 7
The Power of the Mind

January 28: Ouchie update. Well, hi, ladies! I now have a port catheter in my chest with a tube attached to my jugular vein. Not only will they use this to give me the chemo so it won't damage the smaller veins in my arms, but they can draw blood from this, too! I was thinking I'd end up like a pincushion by the end of this ordeal, so while still sore now, it was worth putting it in. I think I may have made a "boo boo" though. I had a ditzy nurse who said I could take the "bandage" off after 24 hours. I kept thinking it was the weirdest bandage I'd ever seen because it was transparent. The doctor who inserted the port cath said he used "superglue" to seal the two incisions, one about 3" long for the big round part and a smaller one to stitch the catheter to the vein. I started to pull off this "transparent bandage" and I think now it must be the superglue stuff! So I put a band-aid over the corner that is torn, and I hope I don't split apart! ☺

The heart test didn't hurt, it just took a long time. First they drew out some blood and mixed it with a radioactive substance, and then I laid on a table with my arms pulled up over my head (and the side where the port cath is is still very sore) and the tech (who couldn't say his "R's" because he had a lisp) brought the machine down over me. It's sort of a tube but not as bad as an MRI. I had to hold still for over 30 minutes and my shoulders started getting twitchy!

He put EKG electrodes on my chest because they time the "pictures" to the beat of your heart. I wish I could have seen them! I asked the tech, and he said, "You'll have to ask the wadiologist." So I didn't see them....

I think all the poking and prodding is finished until Tuesday, when I start the "search and destroy" medicine and then the actual chemo. As long as I focus on the "cool but weird" aspects of this, it's not so scary. I already have a children's book in mind about this...BTW, I'm going to color my hair red tomorrow. I'll try to get a picture and send it to you! If it turns out purple or something weird, it won't matter since it's going to fall out anyway, so I'm going to "experiment."

* * *

I've always been a science nerd, and it came in handy during this time of unfamiliar terminology and procedures. I was able to distance my emotions from what was happening to me so I didn't feel like a trapped lab rat. And, since my "normal" hectic life had been taken from me, I had more time to focus on spiritual things, which was the biggest blessing of all.

"For to set the mind on the flesh is death, but to set the mind on the Spirit is life and peace."

Romans 8:6

Reflection: The human mind, created by God, is a powerful thing. He gave us the will to live, and we can use that strong will to fight the cancer bent on destroying our lives. More importantly, a mind set on the Spirit is able to accomplish amazing things for the Lord and His kingdom.

Chapter 8
Control is an Illusion

January 31: Okay, I lost it! It's a good thing we sit up in the front of the auditorium and that I sit between two very tall men. (Robert is officially 6 feet tall now.) Yesterday the song between the Lord's supper and the sermon was "In Heavenly Love Abiding." Those words have never jumped off the page and struck me like they did yesterday morning:

"In heavenly love abiding, no change my heart shall fear; and safe is such confiding, for nothing changes here. The storm may roar without me, my heart may low be laid, but God is round about me, and can I be dismayed?"

I tried to keep singing, but my voice just choked up and Keith had to hand me his hankie.

I think the hardest lesson for me to learn in all of this is SURRENDER. I didn't realize until recently what a control freak I am, but so much of this is out of my control. I'm having to learn how to have a child-like faith and let God be in total control. He never changes no matter what happens to us here!

Keith and Robert brought me a CD player with headphones to take on Tuesday (since they said plan to be there all day) and I'm bringing my stuffed dog to hold, too. I'll have my Bible and hope that I'll be able to read it! I want to bring it every time, though, just in case one of the other chemo patients has a question, I'll be armed and ready!

All I can say is, "Prepare to die, cancer scum!"

***

My extremely self-sufficient parents taught me to "take charge." As the eldest daughter, it was easy to do just that. I never thought of this trait as a leadership skill. My only thought was to get things done and do them right. I'd heard so many times during my childhood to "Never make a promise you're not willing to honor." If I made a commitment, I'd find a way to keep it, even if it killed me. I guess I was so focused on *doing*, I forgot to look up and remember *who* I was serving.

"Many are the plans in the mind of a man, but it is the purpose of the LORD that will stand."

Proverbs 19:21

Reflection: It's a humbling lesson for a self-reliant person to learn, that control is an illusion. I'm just sorry it took a life-threatening disease for me to truly recognize the fact that God who created the universe and everything in it is the one in control, not me.

Chapter 9
The Power of Prayer

January 31: I have RED hair now! My good friend Cheryl came over tonight and colored my hair what was supposed to be "dark auburn" but it's RED! (Not Lucille Ball red, but lighter than it showed on the box! Sort of an "Anne of Green Gables" red!!!) Robert took a picture, so hopefully it will turn out! He said, "So what if you DON'T lose your hair?" Well, the doctor said I would be bald by David's graduation…

I'm ready to get started on chemo tomorrow! I have complete faith that the Lord will be holding my hand. "Cast thy burden upon the Lord, and He shall sustain thee: He shall never suffer the righteous to be moved." Psalm 55:22 KJV

Thank you for all the prayers. They help so much!

* * *

I never understood the power of prayer until I became the one being prayed for. There were hundreds praying for me around the world, many whom I'd never even met. It was humbling, and I felt lifted on wings of prayer. It gave me so much strength to know so many were presenting my name before the throne of God. I never wanted to forget this blessing so I could pray for others and share it with them.

"Therefore, confess your sins to one another and pray for one another, that you may be healed. The prayer of a righteous person has great power as it is working."

James 5:16

Reflection: We should never underestimate the power of prayer. After all, the omnipotent Father to whom we are praying is able to do more than we can ever imagine.

Chapter 10
Thankful for Every Small Victory

February 1: Grrreat news! My bone marrow is clear! Hallelujah!!! God is good! No more bone marrow biopsies!!!!!!!

I'm finally coming out of my drug-induced haze at 7:30 our time. The nurse said I might have to take Benadryl tonight to get to sleep, though, since I took such a high dose of Prednisone plus an IV steroid. Now that is a weird sensation to feel warm all over because all your vessels are dilated, and you want to jump up and run in a marathon, but your eyes and brain are in a total fog from the IV Benadryl to keep the allergic reaction down. It took from 9 a.m. to 2 p.m. to infuse one bag of Rituxin (the "search and destroy" antibody) because they started out just a drop at a time. I kept falling asleep from the Benadryl and the nurse (Leah, she was wonderful!) said, "Don't fight it, just sleep," but once I woke myself up snoring! The lady sitting across from me tried very hard not to laugh! ☺

The room is not very big, but there are 8-10 recliners in a circle for all the chemo patients with a nurse's station so the two nurses can keep a close eye on everyone. I was the youngest one there today. One man looked close to my age, and 3-4 in the late 50's or early 60's, but the rest were elderly, and some looked downright cadaverous! For once in my life I'm glad I'm overweight so I have some "reserves"!

I didn't get to talk to very many of the patients, since most of us were drowsy. I was glad for my CD player, though—I listened to Baroque (Telemann) and Irish music and some Bach, and I stayed v-e-r-y calm and had no reaction to the medicine. When I was awake I imagined the little "soldier" antibodies hunting down the cancer cells and covering all the lymph nodes! I told the doctor before I left that it must have been my very vivid imagination but I could feel some of the lymph nodes "moving" as if they were cringing at the attack! She said (and the nurse verified it) that this type of lymphoma is very susceptible to the antibody, and that it will actually kill many cells, not just mark them! So I could have felt something "moving" in there! Creepy!!!!!

I hope I didn't ramble on too long here. The actual "chemo" part is on Thursday (3 different drugs). I'm glad the "easier" one was first so I could go through the procedure once. The nurse did leave the drip line in my chest catheter so she wouldn't have to stick me twice in one week; now I'm wired for sound, or maybe some IV orange juice...JK. Thanks again for all your prayers! It helps SO much! There is no One like our God!

* * *

I've had a lot of painful medical procedures over the years, but that bone marrow biopsy was the first one that made me cry out. (I had C-sections after labor but did not deliver a baby, so I probably would have cried out then, too.) For that and many other reasons, I was SO relieved the lymphoma had not invaded the bone marrow!

"I will give thanks to the LORD with my whole heart."

Psalm 9:1

Reflection: In the midst of so much sorrow and bad news, it's especially important to rejoice in "small" victories. It helps keep our mindset as positive as possible, as well as stay focused on the final goal, which is to defeat the Beast.

Chapter 11
Who Stole My Brain?

February 3: First chemo—weird! I will make this short as I have, in my nurse, Leah's words: "chemo brain." I feel very fuzzy, but not the same kind of fuzzy as Tuesday's Benadryl (none of that today, so no snoring, at least! ;)

Leah started my IV line with a "stronger" steroid that she said might keep me awake tonight (I'm so fuzzy I don't see how that will happen at this point) and then directly injected the bright red Adriamycin, which has given me a sinus-type headache (not too bad) and a small amount of Vincristine (which is made from the periwinkle plant) and then "dripped" the Cytoxan. It only took 2 ½ hours today. I just tried to breathe slow and easy while listening to Bach and holding my stuffed puppy that Robert gave me. I thought I would picture this stuff like "pac men" eating the cancer cells, but all I could "see" was flamethrowers!!!! Urban warfare!

When Keith brought me home I ate some applesauce and crackers with peanut butter. Everything has a metallic taste. I've already had two diet 7-ups because I have been feeling "urpy." So far this medicine is keeping it under control, though. I guess the worst is the "fog"—I wasn't expecting that!

I asked about hair loss, and Leah said I would start noticing it next week (already!) and that I could lose it all by the week after the 2nd round (which would be the first of March). She also gave me a shot to help build up the white blood count once it drops. I'll get that checked for the next two Tuesdays.

Robert says he's definitely going to shave his head, so I guess I'll have to get a picture of our bald heads together! That will be very, very weird! Thankfully it's only temporary....Thank you SO much for all the prayers and encouraging words! They have helped me more than I can tell you!

* * *

I expected chemo's more publicized side effects, such as nausea and hair loss. I'd even read something on the internet that claimed a "blood/brain barrier" would keep chemo from affecting the brain. That was NOT the case! The brain fog began almost immediately and made it extremely difficult to think the simplest things. It was like processing thoughts through a filter clogged with globby gelatin.

My mother's solution to chemo brain? "Let's play word games to help you think better." That was like torture to a wordsmith! I couldn't read anything with comprehension, and I couldn't even follow the plot of a movie. I definitely couldn't drive. Even my memories were affected. It was quite shocking, and I wondered if it would ever return to normal.

Thankfully, a few weeks after the last infusion, the fog lifted.

"Even before a word is on my tongue, behold, O LORD, you know it altogether." Psalm 139:4

Reflection: I was so grateful God knew my heart when my brain was so foggy I could hardly think. I had expected to have lots of time for Bible study, but on the worst days, all I could do was lie on the couch and listen to hymns.

Chapter 12
God's Hand through the Fire

February 7: Chemo: The Legend of the Phoenix. Normally our bodies change gradually (unless we get a really strange haircut,) and so we daily adapt to having more gray in our hair or another wrinkle, or a little ache that wasn't there before. We can accept that as the normal part of growing older.

But this chemo stuff is a SLAM WHAM pin your shoulders to the mat, FULL BODY SURFING on a wave of LAVA. I feel every cell in my body turning inside out and melting. I think the "brain fog" has been a blessing in disguise to help me slowly get a handle on what's happening. I don't know how people handle this enormous upheaval without faith in God. Maybe it's not so dramatic for everyone; I hope not! Even my bones feel achy and "melting." I'm supposed to get a blood count tomorrow—I think I still have some! ☺ I have no taste now, but I'm making myself eat. Leah, the nurse says if my mouth hurts too bad she has an anesthetic spray called "pink magic." I wonder why so many things related to chemo are colorful?

Anyway, by the time this "phoenix" rises from the ashes and has to get burned again, I should be better prepared for the next body slam. And if I ever get out of this "brain fog" maybe I can actually write you a coherent message! Please don't stop praying yet!

* * *

This email was much less descriptive than what was actually happening, but I didn't want to scare anyone. What really happened was, within the space of an hour, I felt as if I'd been burned up from the inside out, or turned inside out and shoved through a nuclear reactor. It was such a strong sensation of being on fire, along with feeling bloated with toxic fumes, I got in the shower and stood under the cool water, crying and begging God to stop it. Chemo is deadly poison, and this regimen was worse than most, because lymphoma is difficult to kill. For that horrible hour, it was one breath at a time, one sob at a time, holding onto God because there was nothing else I could do but ride it out. Once the wave finally passed, I felt like a pile of ashes, a phoenix consumed by its own fire.

"When you pass through the waters, I will be with you; and through the rivers, they shall not overwhelm you; when you walk through fire you shall not be burned, and the flame shall not consume you."

Isaiah 43:2

Reflection: I'd heard the expression most of my life: "Take one day at a time." During chemo it often became, "Take one minute at a time." During this particular chemo "wave" effect, it was just me and the fire and the Lord holding me until it passed.

Chapter 13
Love in Action

February 12: Aftershocks. Well, this has been an interesting week. I was averaging 3 hours of sleep a night until last night. I actually got almost 7 hours! Yeah! Maybe the prednisone is FINALLY gone!

I went with Keith and Robert on Thursday to be with the Jones family. (Note: My mother-in-law died on February 8.) I just felt like I needed to be there. My father-in-law is having a hard time, so I got to hug him several times. I had found an 8x10 picture of my mother-in-law from 1969 when she looked gorgeous. She'd given it to me years ago because she didn't want to be reminded of what she used to look like—scleroderma is an awful disease causing hardening of the connective tissues, so although she was only 67 when she died, she looked in her 90's. We got a nice frame for this picture and gave it to my father-in-law, and he was SO pleased! Everyone thought that the picture had been thrown away!

We stayed too late, though, and I was feeling pretty crummy. I thought I had heartburn, but by the time we got home it was feeling like an "aftershock" of the chemotherapy. It felt like a mouse was running around on top of my liver! My stomach bloated just like over the weekend from the chemo!

By morning it had faded, and after a few more "mouse runs" yesterday, I think maybe the aftershocks are finished. I hope so!!! Now I plan to rest and try to get "ready" for the next round of chemo on Feb. 22 & 24.

My friend Cheryl, who colored my hair, has offered to cut it short in the next couple of days. I have never really had short hair, so this will be interesting….I haven't been bald since I was a baby, either, but my mother says I had a cute bald head!

You really find out who your friends are when bad things happen! When the first cards started coming in, I taped them to the back of our front door. That door has already filled up, and now the second door is halfway full! Many of these cards are from Christians I've never met in other parts of the country! And many are from all of you! ☺ You have no idea how much they help—I look at them every day and remember all the prayers being sent my way….It is a real source of strength!

* * *

I had sent cards to people when they were sick, never realizing how much they could help. A card, especially a funny one, or even a brief handwritten note is not just an expression of concern. It's a tangible form of love that tells the sick or suffering person they are important to someone, that they have not been forgotten.

"Little children, let us not love in word or talk but in deed and in truth."

I John 3:18

Reflection: I learned that the small things we do for others are not small at all. They are really the big things. They are love in action.

Chapter 14
When Marriage Vows Become Real

February 16: My hair is really, really short (1/2 inch in back, about an inch on top). It feels really, really weird, but it doesn't look too bad. Yes, it's already falling out which is why I wanted Cheryl to cut it so it won't be so traumatic when it starts coming out in handfuls!

On Sunday night I got all teary eyed talking with my husband, afraid that he will be repulsed by me the uglier I get, and he was so sweet to reassure me. For Valentine's day he got me a new mouse for the computer AND a book of love poems (the first gift is typical of him; the second is not!) And yesterday he took the whole afternoon off so we could get my lab work done (my blood count is back up—yea!!), order a wig, get groceries, and take Robert to get a passport so he can go with Grandpa to England to take his grandmother's ashes back "home." Whew—that wiped me out!

* * *

Keith and I were only twenty years old when we made those vows to one another: "For better, for worse, in sickness and in health...." We had NO idea what we were promising! Now those vows were put to the test, and Keith was a wonderful caregiver. He always drove me to the cancer center for chemo and other appointments. He said we were in this together, and he meant it! My love for him grew by leaps and bounds.

"In the same way husbands should love their wives as their own bodies. He who loves his wife loves himself. For no one ever hated his own flesh, but nourishes and cherishes it, just as Christ does the church."

Ephesians 5:28-29

Reflection: Fighting the Beast together can strengthen a marriage and help love grow to new heights. It's a tremendous confirmation of love and life.

Chapter 15
Preparing for Battle

February 19: Bye, bye, hair! It was inevitable but still creepy....after several days of my scalp feeling "bruised" my hair suddenly started falling out in clumps this morning. I'm SOOOOO glad I had my friend Cheryl cut it short! It's very messy but would have been much worse when it was longer. Hopefully my wig will come in by Monday.... Of course my strange brain is imagining that the reason my scalp has been so sore is that the hair follicles were letting out their last primordial scream as they died.... But, like the phoenix, they shall rise from the ashes! And it will be interesting to see what grows back....

Round 2 of chemo begins Tuesday. Please keep me in your prayers. Now that I know how bad it gets, I'm trying to "gird up the loins of my mind" and remember I Corinthians 16:13—"Watch ye, stand fast in the faith, quit you like men, be strong" and II Timothy 1:7—"For God has not given us the spirit of fear, but of power, and of love, and of a sound mind." KJV So many Scriptures have new meaning for me now!

With sword in one hand and shield in the other,

Katy

* * *

Before I battled the Beast, I didn't understand the phrase in I Peter 1:13 in the old King James about "girding up the loins of your mind." The English Standard Version makes it clearer: "preparing your minds for action." Fighting cancer is a battle and requires mental focus to work WITH the chemo to destroy the invading cells that do NOT want to surrender their host body. In battling this unseen enemy, it also helped me better understand how we battle "the spiritual forces of evil in the heavenly places" — with God's power, not our own.

"Therefore take up the whole armor of God, that you may be able to withstand in the evil day, and having done all, to stand firm."

Ephesians 6:13

Reflection: As a soldier prepares for war with training and setting his mind for the coming fight, so does a cancer patient. Both mirror the spiritual warfare a Christian wages with the ever-present help of God.

Chapter 16
Losing My Glory

February 22: Call me Baldy, and good news. This morning I took a shower before going to the cancer center and when I washed my hair it POURED off my head! I literally had a huge pile of hair in my hands! There were just three or four straggling strands left hanging on for dear life! So Keith shaved them off for me a little while ago. Boy does my head look smaller (and there's a draft)! Keith also shaved Robert's head, and we got a picture of our two cueballs. ☺ Hopefully it will turn out! Keith bought me FIVE hats at Wal-Mart (cheap and colorful) since my wig hasn't come in yet (hopefully Thursday). When I'm finished with the hats, I can donate them to the "pile" at the cancer center.

The good news is that the doctor said "go ahead" on my recommended dose of prednisone! Yeah! Instead of 100 mg for five days and quitting "cold turkey," I can take it 100-80-60-40-20 and maybe it won't be so bad the second week—maybe I'll even sleep more!!!! Isn't that pathetic when you can get so excited about a change in medication dosage! Ha!

The "marker drug" went in fine today with no reaction (I went in at 9:00 am and was finished by 2:00 pm). I did doze off from the IV Benadryl and did NOT wake myself up snoring this time! I even wrote part of a scene from a Texas novel I'm desperately trying to finish. I say "part" because some of the sentences trail off into nonsense, when I was dozing off, I guess. I get a CT scan in two weeks, and my doctor is hoping I will only have the four total treatments and be finished because she said the lymph nodes were "significantly smaller after just one treatment"—yeah!!!

* * *

One of the few times I shed tears during this ordeal was that moment my hair poured off my head. It had been bad enough to cut it short, but to lose it like that was a shock. I'd had long hair most of my life and it really had become my "glory." I didn't mind the feel of a bald head, but I could hardly bear to look at myself in the mirror. It was difficult to see a woman in that reflection when it looked more like a Galapagos tortoise!

"He alone is my rock and my salvation, my fortress; I shall not be greatly shaken."

Psalm 62:2

Reflection: The rapid physical changes caused by chemotherapy were unsettling and caused mental and emotional upheaval and depression, despite my attempt at being cheerful in the emails. Having hats and wigs to hide behind helped me put on a brave face. Knowing God was my Rock gave me something unchanging to cling to.

Chapter 17

The Hour of Dread

February 25: Round 2 & I have a wig now. It sure is hard to RELAX when you know poison is going into your body, but that's what I tried to do yesterday and imagine it killing the cancer cells. Today I have the usual "fog" and nausea and headache, but I'm staying up with the meds and it's helping a lot. Keith came home for lunch and took me to pick up my wig. I feel like a woman again instead of a bald turtle! ☺ I can't tell you enough how much your prayers mean to me! Thanks from the bottom of my socks!

* * *

Before the second round began, I dreaded the return of that hour when the awful poison would burn me up from the inside and turn me into the mythical phoenix once more. As I tried to explain to others, it wasn't fear or a lack of faith, because I had no fear of dying. Because I'd experienced the "chemo wave" and now knew what was coming, I totally dreaded the return of suffering.

Only then did I begin to understand a little of what Jesus felt while He prayed in the Garden of Gethsemane. He prayed in agony, knowing the excruciating pain He would experience in the next several hours of abuse, scourging, and crucifixion. But He looked beyond the suffering to the joy that would follow: His resurrection and the gift of salvation now available to all because of His willingness to endure.

"And being in anguish, he prayed more earnestly, and his sweat was like drops of blood falling to the ground."

Luke 22:44

"For the joy set before him he endured the cross, scorning its shame, and sat down at the right hand of the throne of God."

Hebrews 12:2

Reflection: Hope that chemo would put the cancer in remission became my focus beyond the suffering of the "chemo wave". Now that I'd begun to better understand the anguish Jesus suffered for us all, I could be comforted in my hour of dread.

Chapter 18
Producing Steadfastness

March 1: Better & Worser. Yes, I know that's not a word, but after all I have my "poetic license." ☺ Tapering off the prednisone dose seems to have lessened the "nuclear reactor" effects of the chemo, and so far I don't have the horrible jitters that I did last time! Yeah! But I'm up at 1:30 a.m. because my bones feel "sore" which probably means a low blood count. I have been feeling extremely fatigued, which goes along with it, too. Please pray that my count today isn't dangerously low, and if so that The Shot can bring it back up in time for the next chemo round. (When the nurses say "The Shot" it sounds like they're saying it with capital letters!) There is so much flu going around, I sure don't want to catch any yucky bugs right now!

Thank you for your love and prayers. I have been so humbled and gratified to know that so many are praying! It really helps focus on what's truly important....

* * *

One of many unexpected things about chemotherapy was how helpless the treatment made me feel. It is deadly poison, after all, killing more than just the cancerous cells. All fast-growing cells, such as blood, hair, and the lining of the digestive tract, are susceptible to the chemo.

I lost every hair on my body, but that paled in comparison to the other effects. At the lowest point in each round, I felt more dead than alive. The low red cell count made it difficult to do anything, even walk down the hall to the bathroom, because the lack of oxygen made me so short of breath. The low white count made me anxious that I had almost NO defenses against any kind of virus or infection going around. My mouth was so full of sores it hurt to eat or drink anything. And the weird and painful things chemo did to my digestive tract made me not want to put anything else in my body. Compared to how active I had been, I felt useless.

In one of life's little ironies, the chore I'd always hated most—ironing—now became the only chore I could reliably manage. I had to sit on a stool because I hadn't the strength to stand, and I didn't move very fast, but it gave me a sense of accomplishment to iron Keith's clothes every day.

"Count it all joy, my brothers, when you meet trials of various kinds, for you know that the testing of your faith produces steadfastness."

James 1:2-3

Reflection: I never understood how "joy" and "trials" could be used in the same sentence until I experienced chemo. Only then did I understand the joy doesn't happen *while* the painful things are happening. The joy comes from the steadfastness produced as a result of endurance *through* the trials. The joy is in seeing God more clearly by burning away some of the inconsequential matters of this life that once seemed so important.

Chapter 19
Practicing Good Medicine

March 1: Two posts in one day---sorry! I didn't want to leave you all hanging. My red count is only slightly down, but my white count is WAY down, which accounts for the way I'm feeling right now. I have to stay away from people and The Shot should bring it back up by the end of the week. My fever was 100, so the doctor prescribed a "mild" antibiotic to help. Thank you for the prayers!!!!

I wore my wig to the cancer center and all the nurses said they loved it. Dr. B hollered into the hallway, "Get this girl a microphone and she can be Loretta Lynn!" Yes, it's pretty curly! ☺

* * *

Looking back, I know that wig must have looked a bit ridiculous. It was close to my color (dark brown) but curlier than my hair had ever been. It did make me feel better to wear it, though. And everyone at the cancer center was kind to say they "loved" it.

Dr. B, especially, had learned how important it is for her patients to be surrounded by loving care, kind words, and humor. She never married or had children. Instead, she has devoted her life to defeating the Beast at every opportunity. How she manages to stay so upbeat despite losing many of her beloved patients never ceases to amaze me. Her sense of humor sustains her as well as her patients.

"A joyful heart is good medicine, but a crushed spirit dries up the bones."

Proverbs 17:22

Reflection: Being able to find the humor, even dark humor, in a difficult situation like cancer and chemo can ease the burden, not only for ourselves but for everyone around us. Science has documented the benefits of laughter to our physical and mental well-being, but God knew it first.

Chapter 20
Strange Weapons

March 15: "Good" chemo stays true to its name! I'm sitting here wired up for Thursday. It's kind of like having a straw in your chest—wish they could put in some lemonade or root beer instead! The "good" chemo went in with no problems—whew! The nurse had told me that sometimes it will still have a reaction later in the series, but this time it behaved. Good chemo! Here's your doggie treat! I arranged my pillow so my head wouldn't fall back when I fell asleep during the Benadryl "wave" so I don't think I snored. The man across from me did a couple of times! He's the one that sometimes wears bright green alligator skin cowboy boots….

The CAT scan showed the mass in my neck much, much smaller! The doctor said she knew the lymph nodes would be smaller, but this was even better than she hoped for after just two rounds! I'll have another one after the 4th round which will show for sure whether or not we can stop at four! That's my hope and prayer!!!! I'm going to enjoy the rest of today and tomorrow before the "slam" on Thursday. Thank you for your prayers!!!

P.S. When they start the IV on this Rituxan (the "search and destroy" one) I picture little guys in camouflage floating through my bloodstream with their infrared lights and Uzis! Yes, I know I'm weird!

* * *

It's interesting how the strangest things can be the most helpful in one's fight against the Beast. For me, the stuffed dog Robert gave me accompanied me to every appointment and infusion. Like my three-year-old self clutching a blanket, that little dog reminded me I was loved and prayed for and gave me something tangible to hold onto in a time of constant unknown terrors.

And like my fellow patient who always wore his green boots, I found something to wear that gave me more courage on especially scary days: a short, sassy red wig! Who would have thought a wig like that could be more effective at chasing away fear than wearing a Samurai mask?

The other technique I read about, which comes to me naturally as a writer, is visualization or guided imagery. There is some evidence that using the imagination to help fight the Beast is effective, even if it only helps relax the patient so the chemo can do its work. Picturing little Special Forces warriors swarming through my veins also gave me the illusion of being able to DO something rather than passively receive the treatment.

"For you equipped me with strength for the battle."

Psalm 18:39

Reflection: Prayer is a most powerful weapon, a tremendous blessing from God. But we should not overlook any available resource to add to our arsenal, no matter how insignificant it may at first appear.

Chapter 21
Renewing Determination

March 20: #3 crash & burn. This chemo is really strange—just when you think you have it figured out, it pulls the rug out from under you! #1 was like a nuclear reactor, but #2 was much easier with the lower dose of prednisone. My nurse did tell me that it tends to get a little worse each time, but it wasn't "worse" until yesterday (Saturday) when I felt that nuclear reactor stuff again, like you're being burned from the inside out. My bones are all melty and achy, two days earlier than last time, which means the white blood count is dropping. The good thing is that these cancer cells no longer "scream"—they just "whimper." They don't have much fight left in 'em! But I DO! And I'm not stopping until every last cell is GONE! I think I'm going to lose the eyebrows this round—I may have to hire Robert to "draw" them—ha!

* * *

Even with the built-in recovery time, each round of chemo is worse than the one before. The poisons have a cumulative effect on the body. After all, if too much time passes between infusions, the cancer has opportunity to multiply and mutate, which makes the chemo no longer effective.

This means, unfortunately, that the good cells don't have enough time to completely heal before they're slammed again.

The body's ability to heal is incredible. The tricky part for a cancer patient is to be as resilient as possible—roll with the punches and not let the discomfort distract you from the main goal. At times it feels like you've lost when the chemo knocks you flat. One round is only one battle in the overall war. In war there are casualties and collateral damage, but they alone can't keep an army from winning the war in the end.

"We rejoice in our sufferings, knowing that suffering produces endurance, and endurance produces character, and character produces hope."

Romans 5:3-4

Reflection: Cancer is a ferocious enemy. It won't be easily defeated, but neither will we, if we put our hope and trust in God and take this opportunity to grow mightily in faith.

Chapter 22
Sentenced to Jail

March 22: Hello, I'm neutropenic—how 'bout you? Well, I am totally bummed. My white blood count is even lower this time than last time! That explains the fevers and chills I've been having, and the fact that my bones "hurt" more than usual. My sweet nurse said "Guess what? You're neutropenic," as if it were a good thing! She says everything sweetly, though. She really is a wonderful person! Neutropenia is just a fancy medical word for low white blood count, but I think she meant that it explained my symptoms. I don't fault her! I just feel like I've been sentenced to jail! I can't go anywhere until my blood is checked again next week, and we have a gospel meeting this weekend I really wanted to go to.

I am thankful for Maalox. The heartburn has started earlier this time, and I haven't been eating much or drinking enough (bad, I know) because it feels like I have holes in my stomach. The only thing that tastes good right now, besides macaroni & cheese, is a milkshake, but I don't want to get used to eating THOSE. ☺ Would you please pray that my white count will come back up by next week so I'll be ready for the 4th (and hopefully final) round of chemo the first week of April???

Okay, enough whining. For every good cell the chemo kills, it is SLAMMING the few remaining cancer cells....If I can just keep that in mind, I can handle being "trapped" at home for a week....

***

There is a difference between feeling so sick you don't want to go anywhere and being told you CAN'T go anywhere because your immune system is dangerously low. I felt like a small child being told I couldn't do something, which of course made me want to do it all the more.

I didn't get terribly sick this round, but the last round my white count went down almost as far as it could go, and I contracted a bad lung infection. Only then did I find out some people have to be hospitalized and quarantined during chemo when their immune systems bottom out. Finally, I realized how this week of "involuntary incarceration" had been a small price to pay.

What did the Apostle Paul do when he was imprisoned? Whine and complain about how unfair it was? No, I was humbled to remember. In Philippians, he talked about joy!

"Rejoice in hope, be patient in tribulation, be constant in prayer."
Romans 12:12

Reflection: No matter how discouraging everything seems to be, there is always something for which to give thanks. A heart of gratitude can make everything look brighter.

Chapter 23
What Love Looks Like

March 24: I've got to tell you what my son Robert did. He won't turn fifteen until the end of April, so he can't drive yet. We ran out of macaroni & cheese, and since it's almost the only thing I can eat right now, he walked more than a mile each way to the nearest store, just so he could make some for me! When he got home he said he was disappointed no one stopped him. I thought he meant to give him a ride, but he said, "No! Two different police cars drove right by me and didn't ask, 'Why aren't you in school?' I wanted them to ask me so I could say, 'I'm homeschooled, and my mom has cancer and all she can eat is mac & cheese, so I went to get her some.'" Isn't that funny and sweet?

* * *

The entire three months of chemo, I was enveloped in love. One homeschooling Mom set up a schedule so those from our group as well as ladies from church could bring our family regular meals. Cards and gifts arrived almost daily. Since I couldn't meet with my bi-monthly writer's critique group in San Antonio, one lady sent handwritten notes along with her current writing project, asking my opinion as if it were still valuable.

Keith continued to take off work so he could drive me to appointments. And Robert, who was already a compassionate soul, took his role as caregiver seriously. Before cancer, I looked forward to the monthly Boy Scout campouts as my "alone time" to binge write in the peace and quiet, since Keith was a troop leader and accompanied Robert.

Now that I knew how fragile life could be, I no longer looked forward to their absence. I treasured every moment with them. I never again wanted to take their love, or anyone else's, for granted. And I was determined to better demonstrate my love for others.

"Little children, let us not love in word or talk but in deed and in truth."

I John 3:18

Reflection: When we show our love to others by our actions, we can be a reflection of God's great love for us.

Chapter 24
Getting Restless

March 29: Going up, going down. I got my blood checked today—the white cell count is coming back up, but the red blood count and platelets are low! So now Katy-the-Klutz has to be extra careful. Hmmm….no fencing, no knife-throwing, no cutting up carrots, even! (And no opening pop-top cans, either—I still have a nice arrow-shaped scar from that last visit to ER…)

I did write a limerick:

There once was a flutist named Newt
So incredibly bored with his flute
That all in one day
He forgot how to play
And instead learned to pluck on a lute.

I'm not bored with my flute, though! I miss playing it and plan to practice a lot more once I'm able! Next week is round #4 and HOPEFULLY the last one, but I won't know until after the next CT scan.

* * *

It's amazing how much we take for granted until we lose it. The most basic things, like breathing, eating, sleeping, and walking become difficult during chemo. Even though I didn't practice daily, I knew after playing for 35 years that I could pick up my flute at any time and play it with no problem.

Not so when my mouth was full of sores because every tiny nick became infected, and my breathing was labored because of a low red count. Even my fingers were shaky when I tried to hold the instrument.

Thankfully, the last week before the next round I could usually do a few normal things. By sitting on a stool instead of standing, I managed to keep my homeschool biology class going as well as the homeschool band. The students just had to do their part at home when I couldn't breathe the same air with them. By the end of May, I was able to direct the band in a Star Wars concert and take the biology class on a field trip to the Corpus Christi Aquarium. Both wiped me out but felt like huge accomplishments!

"But they who wait for the LORD shall renew their strength; they shall mount up with wings like eagles; they shall run and not be weary; they shall walk and not faint."

Isaiah 40:31

Reflection: One of the most difficult and important lessons to learn through chemo is patience. An overly busy person like me especially needed to remember the words of Jesus, "Peace, be still."

Chapter 25
Encouragement

April 4: I got to go to services yesterday! When I get through this, I am going to try very hard not to take anything for granted again—like worshipping on the Lord's day!!! On Saturday I was feeling pretty low—physically and mentally. My allergies have been acting up big-time and I haven't felt "ready" for round four starting tomorrow. But after going to both services and Bible class yesterday, I feel like my batteries have been recharged! ☺ It was the first Sunday I'd been able to go in three weeks.

We sang a song Sunday morning that I've sung for years, but the words never meant what they do now:

> Amid the trials which I meet,
> Amid the thorns which pierce my feet,
> One thought remains supremely sweet,
> Thou thinkest, Lord, of me!
>
> The cares of life come thronging fast,
> Upon my soul their shadow cast;
> Their gloom reminds my heart at last,
> Thou thinkest, Lord, of me!
>
> Let shadows come, let shadows go,
> Let life be bright or dark with woe,
> I am content, for this I know,
> Thou thinkest, Lord, of me!

> Thou thinkest, Lord of me,
> Thou thinkest, Lord, of me,
> What need a I fear when Thou art near
> And thinkest, Lord of me.

"O Lord, thou hast searched me, and known me." Psalm 139:1 KJV (Actually this whole Psalm is totally cool!) Have a wonderful day, ladies!

* * *

Another thing I'd always taken for granted was the ability to attend worship services with the local church. Now I better understood the plight of the "shut-ins" who were willing but no longer able to go. It's a huge blessing to worship God together with brothers and sisters in Christ. God designed the church in part as a way for members to build up one another. When we miss the services, no matter what the reason, we miss the opportunity to encourage others and be encouraged in return.

A few said they were surprised to see me when I was feeling so badly, but they added it was an encouragement to them to see how important the worship service was to me. Until that moment I didn't realize I could be a good example to others in that way. I was only remembering how an elderly member always encouraged me by his faithful attendance, even though I knew he lived with almost constant pain.

Four synonyms of encouragement are: inspiration, motivation, stimulation, fortification.

"Let us consider how to stir up one another to love and good works, not neglecting to meet together, as is the habit of some, but encouraging one another."

Hebrews 10:24-25

Reflection: Knowing how the encouragement of others can build us up and inspire us to do better, we should not neglect any opportunity to do the same for them.

Chapter 26
Plans

April 5: My red count was still low, which explains why I've been so short of breath and my heart's been racing—not enough red blood cells carrying enough oxygen so my heart and lungs are working harder. Despite this, I did my "good" chemo today—no bad reactions—whew!!! I got an extra big dose of The Shot to help the red cells grow faster—there's another one I'll get on Thursday for the white cells.

I'm okay—we have a plan! I'll have another CT scan and a PET scan which uses radioactive glucose to find cancer cells sometime the week of April 18th and then I'll see the doctor on the 26th to get the final word as to whether this is the last round. However, even if I need another round or two, the doctor promised we could wait until I get back from Florida so I can DEFINITELY go see David graduate from college on May 5th—yeah!!!! That way I'd have two extra weeks to recover. I hope I'm making sense!

So even if this round on Thursday slams me to the mat (or knocks me off the mat or shoves me under the mat), I'll have more time to recover, no matter what happens! That is such a relief to know! Thank you for your prayers!!!!!!!

Love, Katy (Anemic, Bald, but still Crazy!) ☺

P.S. As they were dripping the "marker" drug today I "told" my little camo guys (that's how I imagine this stuff works) that this was their most difficult and important mission—there were far fewer cancer cells to find but they were to look in every nook and cranny and not overlook a single one!!!! We want that PET scan to be completely clean! (I watched Robert and his friends playing video games yesterday evening and I think my imagination has really run away with me!)

* * *

I am like my father in that I like to have a PLAN of action. As long as the goal is before me and there are things I can do to meet that goal, I am less likely to give in to anxiety. Note: I did not say I never get anxious, unfortunately. Plans, of course, can be thwarted, but if we put our trust in the Lord, we can find peace in Him that can't be found anywhere else.

The knowledge that even if I needed more than four rounds, I could have those extra two weeks to grow stronger, made my anxiety drain away. I find that the more I worry, the less I pray. And, the more I pray, the less room in my thoughts for worry.

"Do not be anxious about anything, but in everything by prayer and supplication with thanksgiving let your requests be made known to God. And the peace of God, which surpasses all understanding, will guard your hearts and your minds in Christ Jesus."

Philippians 4:6-7

Reflection: It's good to think ahead, but not to the point of obsessing over your plans and forgetting to allow for God's will.

Chapter 27
Death and Life

April 8: Chia pet head & stronger meds. Since I started feeling the "urps" while the chemo was going in yesterday, my nurse gave me samples of a stronger anti-nausea medication, and it works great! I can drink more water and eat a little more, even though I can't taste any of it! My brain fog is still pretty fuzzy but I can think a little better than yesterday, so that's progress!

I think there must be very few cancer cells left. I can't even feel a whimper out of them! I think they're all ready to surrender, even though I told my camo guys to take NO prisoners! No quarter! No mercy!

Keith rubbed my head the other day while I had my thin cotton "night cap" on and started laughing. I said, "What's so funny?" And he said, "Your head feels like a chia pet." Too bad we can't pour some water on it and grow grass or something, huh? Actually I'm okay with the "feel" of my head, it's just the sight in the mirror that I haven't been able to get used to—it still reminds me of a wizened little turtle! ☺

Love, Katy the Chia Turtle

* * *

This fourth round was definitely the worst of the series. All the previous effects were multiplied, but I kept clinging to God's hand through my pain and my tears. I kept praying that this was the last round, that the cancer cells were indeed all dead, since I could no longer feel anything from them.

The color of my skin became weird this round, a sort of yellowish gray, sickly in appearance. I spent many days on the sofa beside the living room window, having no energy and a mostly non-functioning brain. We had identified the bird singing from the bush outside the window as a Carolina wren. I listened to his singing every day, imagining him flitting around, chasing bugs. That little bird was a good reminder of the new life blossoming outside, and I hoped to be able to enjoy it soon.

Something wonderful grew from the wren's song: my first published novel entitled *Leandra's Enchanted Flute*. A Carolina wren named Songcatcher is a major character in this fantasy story about a fourteen-year-old girl who plays flute and has survived cancer.

"This is my comfort in my affliction, that your promise gives me life."

Psalm 119:50

Reflection: I learned through the multiple distresses of chemotherapy that God is always with me and has been my entire life. Being the hard-headed German I've always been, I don't think I could have learned this so personally and so vividly any other way.

Chapter 28
Into the Darkness

April 12: Slam with both barrels….Well at least there's a good reason I feel like I've been hit by a truck! Not only is my white count the lowest it's been, but my red count is low, too! At least the platelets aren't low, but since I just don't have the energy to juggle knives or Ninja throwing stars right now, I guess I'll wait until another day for that….

While my nurse (Helen from the Midwest—she sounds just like Suze!) was taking my blood, she asked me, "What has been the most traumatic thing about chemo?" And I told her, "Losing my normal life." My life was definitely too hectic, but I kinda liked it! Helen said most people think the hair loss is going to be the worst, and then they find out it's really trivial. It is! But the good side is: every moment with your family and friends becomes precious; what seemed to be important really isn't; eternity with God becomes REAL, not just "someday in the far distant future, maybe."

I cannot imagine there is even a single cancer cell left! Will know for sure on the 26th. I got the instructions for the "PET" scan today—sounds different! I have to allow two to three hours for the appointment and eat a special diet for twenty-four hours before (no sugar or carbs) since they're injecting radioactive glucose to find out if there's even one cancer cell in there….

Well, I'm going back to the sofa where I've been "camped" since last Thursday….

* * *

Sometimes it's difficult to see anything good, especially when you're living moment by moment consumed by every kind of discomfort. There are dark times, darker than any you've experienced before. You may even wonder if it wouldn't be easier to quit fighting and let God take you.

Then, in a moment of clarity, you see a ray of hope, and you know with a certainty you've never felt before that no matter what happens next, any suffering in this life is not worth comparing to heaven's glory. Romans 8:18 never felt so real and personal before.

But that's what this whole journey has become — one moment of clarity after another. A staircase to heaven.

"Rejoice not over me, O my enemy; when I fall, I shall rise; when I sit in darkness, the LORD will be a light to me."

Micah 7:8

Reflection: Sometimes we don't realize how bright God's light is until we experience darkness. Then the contrast is unmistakable. Truth that was once nebulous becomes piercingly clear.

Chapter 29
Waiting is SO Hard!

April 19: I've always been an overachiever, but this is a bit ridiculous. On the instructions for the PET scan, it said if my blood sugar was over 80, they couldn't do the test. So instead of doing low carbs for the twenty-four hours before, I did NO carbs. When the tech pricked my finger for the glucose test, it was 65. No wonder I was feeling so shaky!

The PET scan happens in a mobile unit from San Antonio. After the tech checks the blood sugar, he injects radioactive glucose, and you have to rest in a recliner for forty minutes or so to let it search for cancer cells to attach to. Then you lay on a narrow bed and have to remain perfectly still while the imaging machine clicks and whirs and scans your body v-e-r-y slowly (it's MUCH slower than a CT scan). At one point it came so close to my face, I had to close my eyes and go to a happy place. Good thing I'm not claustrophobic.

I'm disappointed I won't get to see the doctor on the 26th but will have to wait until the 29th. She wanted to make sure all the test results came in on time. Ten days seems like such a long way away!

* * *

I once worked in a radiology department, so I knew why technicians aren't allowed to give out information to the patients they are scanning. But surely the guy could see whether or not there was any cancer left. In Dr. B's words, any malignant cells would light up the PET scan screen "like a Christmas tree." But, no. A radiologist has to read it and send his or her report to the doctor. Then the doctor has to compile this report with the coming CT scan report and the bloodwork to make her final determination. I understood that with my head, but boy, was it difficult to be patient!

I felt like a defendant waiting on the jury's ruling. Guilty or not guilty? Go free or continue chemo? If I felt better, I could have kept myself busy with something to pass the time. Instead, I needed to keep praying and waiting and hoping.

"I wait for the LORD, my soul waits, and in his word I hope."

Psalm 130:5

Reflection: Having to wait for momentous news is a good reminder that there will always be things over which we have no control. The best thing to do is to wait — patiently.

Chapter 30
Understanding = Compassion

April 21: I've never wanted to punch someone in the face until today! I was scheduled to have my CT scan at the hospital radiology department. Since they were busy, they sent me to the cardiac cath lab so someone there could start my IV. I was feeling really weak from this lingering lung infection, so I was waiting in a wheelchair, and I currently am bald with no hair anywhere on my body (no eyebrows or eyelashes). A young, impatient tech from the cath lab came to start the IV. He SHOVED the needle into my hand and I yelped, I was so startled (and it did hurt), and he said, "Don't be a wimp!"

If my brain wasn't so fuzzy from the chemo, I would have said something, but he was gone before I could even process his insensitive words. I wish now I had told someone about it!

* * *

Unlike the chemo nurses who see cancer patients every day and have learned how to deal with them, other medical personnel reacted in two basic ways. Most of them were syrupy sweet and treated you like broken glass, but a few were brusque. I wasn't sure if that was because cancer is such a scary word and they wanted to keep themselves as far away from it as possible, or if it was their usual way with patients. This tech was the only overtly rude one, thankfully. It made me wish everyone who treated cancer patients could be sick for just an hour or two so they could truly understand how it felt.

Compassion is a balancing act, especially when dealing with a cancer patient. I had no understanding of what a survivor deals with until I went through it. The physical helplessness, the sickness of chemo poisoning, and the mental effects of losing the normality of life are profound, but a patient fighting cancer doesn't want or need contempt, condescension, or pity. Especially not pity.

"There is one whose rash words are like sword thrusts, but the tongue of the wise brings healing."

Proverbs 12:18

Reflection: A warrior needs courage, and courage can be imparted with something as simple as a smile while making eye contact. Though our bodies may look half-dead, there's still a human being inside, fighting to defeat the Beast and return to life.

Chapter 31
About Chemotherapy

April 26: Blood counts very slowly coming back up. I'm still running a temperature, so started another antibiotic. While waiting in the chemo room for blood counts, the oncology pharmacist (who everyone calls the bartender) wasn't busy, so being the curious person I am, I asked about how he makes his "cocktails." He showed me the area where he mixes the chemicals (poisons). The fumes are so toxic, he uses a vent hood. And he wears gloves. He must be careful not to spill one drop on himself, because it would eat away his skin. Some are more toxic than others, he said. Wow, I never thought of using "pharmacist" and "thrill-seeker" in the same sentence, but working with these chemicals requires nerves of steel!

So, if the chemo drugs will eat through skin, and even the fumes are toxic, why don't they eat through our blood vessels??? One of the chemo nurses did tell me they are hard on the veins.

* * *

I was told chemotherapy was developed from mustard gas, a deadly chemical used in World War I which killed thousands of soldiers in a horrible way. But after looking through medical records of soldiers who survived mustard gas poisoning, two doctors wondered if the same chemical that killed white blood cells might also kill cancer cells that affect the blood, namely leukemia and lymphoma.

The first recorded chemotherapy patient was a man with terminal lymphoma. Desperate indeed to let himself be injected with mustard gas! But it did kill the lymphoma without killing him.

I sometimes wonder if medicine will progress in a few decades to the point where patients will only have to swallow a pill, and the cancer will be killed without harming any innocent cells. Will doctors then talk about the "dark ages" of cancer treatment, when patients used to suffer needlessly from the effects of deadly poisons injected into their veins?

"Fear not, for I am with you; be not dismayed, for I am your God; I will strengthen you, I will help you, I will uphold you with my righteous right hand."

Isaiah 41:10

Reflection: I know not every cancer patient chooses to submit to chemotherapy, and in fact some well-meaning people tried to talk me out of it. But since my lymphoma had grown for so long before being correctly diagnosed, I didn't want to take a chance on a less-proven weapon. Chemotherapy has a long track record of killing lymphoma. It was my choice to use it. In the end, it has to be the patient's choice, and others need to respect that.

Chapter 32
Anticipation and Anxiety

April 28: I check my temperature daily, and it's finally getting back to normal. Between the antibiotics and The Shot, I'm hopeful my white count is on the way up.

Tomorrow I see the doctor and get the verdict. I'm just as nervous as if I were on trial! Will I be found innocent and set free, or guilty and have my sentence extended??? Please pray that if the news is NOT what I want to hear, that I will accept it, and with the two extra weeks of recovery, I can be ready to face more rounds of chemo.

I'll let you know as soon as I hear tomorrow!!!!!! Thank you so much for your prayers!

* * *

Boy, is it HARD to stay calm when you're waiting for news that will determine whether or not you will face more rounds of chemo. Even though you know with your rational mind that anxiety doesn't make anything easier, the "what if's" fill your head and you can't think about anything else.

It's a million times more intense than the feelings I had as a child on Christmas Eve. Not only am I anticipating possible good news, but I am prepared to hear the worst news, too. And I know if it IS bad news, it will feel worse than the initial diagnosis, because now I know exactly what will happen next.

This is, in a way, the most difficult night of the entire battle.

"You keep him in perfect peace whose mind is stayed on you, because he trusts in you."

Isaiah 26:3

Reflection: If we can keep our focus on the Lord and all He has done for us, we can chase away some of the anxiety about the future. After all, He holds the future and is already prepared. Who better to place our trust?

Chapter 33
How Do You Spell Relief?

April 29, 2005: Rejoice with me, ladies!!!!! I am cancer-free!!!!!!!!!!!!!! Well, the technical term is "remission," which means there is no sign of a single cancer cell, but I'll take it!!!!!!!!!!!!!!!!!!

The doctor said the PET scan did show some "Christmas tree" activity in my lungs, but she says it was from the infection I got when my white count was near zero, NOT cancer.

If I had the energy to do a cartwheel, I would! (Even though I've never been able to do one in my life! Ha, ha…..)

I can't tell you how RELIEVED I am that I don't have to have any more chemo!!!!!!!!!!!!!!!!!!

Thank you, THANK YOU all for all the prayers you offered on my behalf, and all the cards and gifts and the many, many ways you showed your love during this terrible time. I don't know how I could have done it without you!!!!

With all my love,

Katy

* * *

When Dr. B grabbed my hand and looked into my eyes, for a second I panicked, thinking she was preparing me to hear bad news. But then she grinned and said, "You're in remission!" I nearly fainted from relief! It felt as if a boulder had fallen from my shoulders.

I hadn't cried when given the diagnosis, but now I did cry. Dr. B said, "Those are happy tears, aren't they?"

"Of course they are." All the way out the door I praised God, over and over!

"You have turned for me my mourning into dancing; you have loosed my sackcloth and clothed me with gladness, that my glory may sing your praise and not be silent. O LORD my God, I will give thanks to you forever!"

Psalm 30:11-12

Reflection: I had never felt such joy and relief at hearing those three blessed words, "You're in remission." The Beast was defeated. After focusing on the fight for so long, I had to scramble to shift my thinking into a different gear, that of recovery and getting back to living.

Afterwards

Keith, Robert and I did fly to Tampa, Florida to see David get his bachelor's degree. I made the mistake of sitting in a backwards-facing seat on the plane. A direct flight would have been no problem, but we had two brief stops—Dallas and New Orleans—and the take-off and landing from that position made me nauseous! I grabbed the "barf bag" but thankfully didn't have to use it.

The wig was hot in Florida, so the day we walked along the beach, I only wore a hat, praying it wouldn't blow off! It was an exhausting trip, but so satisfying on so many levels.

About two weeks later, my foggy chemo brain had vanished, so I started driving again. I took Robert and four other students from my homeschool biology class on an overnight trip to Corpus Christi to the Texas State Aquarium. Again, it was too hot to wear a wig, so I had to hold onto my floppy hat in the stiff breeze coming from the Gulf of Mexico. Looking back, that was pretty brave for me to drive with five lively teens four hours each way and stay the night! I was anxious to get back into life.

I began to heal right away, but mentally I felt a pall over me that I didn't understand. I'd beaten the Beast! I was in remission! So why did I feel so depressed? Dr. B explained that the mental strain of fighting cancer and the physical effects of chemo were so traumatic, I had clinical depression. She prescribed a low dose of Zoloft, which did help. Within a year, I felt like I no longer needed the anti-depressant, so I stopped taking it.

Regarding my new hair: I worried I'd look like a Marine recruit the rest of my life. It was very short for about four months, but then it suddenly started growing quickly, forming tight curls. My hair had been wavy before but never curly. The longer it grew, I kept expecting the curls to relax, but they continued to grow into Shirley Temple ringlets. I asked Dr. B if she'd put Miracle Grow in my chemo!

I had three month checkups for the first year, and beginning with the second year of remission, I had six month checkups. After three years Dr. B said I could have my port catheter removed if I wanted to, explaining that if the lymphoma was going to come back, it tended to recur within the first three years. Although I was a bit nervous about taking out the port, I took a leap of faith.

There was always the shadow of recurrence hanging over my head, and before each checkup I would become very anxious for about a week, wondering if the rug would be pulled out from under my feet again. I've learned from other survivors that it is a common anxiety to have. It's one thing to be ignorant of what's going to happen and quite another to KNOW how cancer treatment will affect you.

The important thing to remember is, you have battled the Beast and won this war. Life becomes precious, every moment of it. We've been spared; we've been blessed. Now it's time to pay it forward and live a meaningful life every step of the way, giving thanks to God for His mercy.

For More Info

Here are some sites with useful information:

National Cancer Institute
https://www.cancer.gov

American Cancer Society
https://www.cancer.org

Leukemia & Lymphoma Society
https://www.lls.org

Katy Huth Jones' Blog: Life is a Four-Letter Word
http://katyhuthjones.blogspot.com

CPSIA information can be obtained
at www.ICGtesting.com
Printed in the USA
LVHW041410070423
743785LV00017B/104